D0848527

HOW DO WE LIVE TOGETHER?
DEER

BY LUCIA RAATMA

CHERRY LAKE
Publishing

Published in the United States of America by Cherry Lake Publishing
Ann Arbor, Michigan
www.cherrylakepublishing.com

Content Adviser: Stephen S. Ditchkoff, PhD, Associate Professor, School of Forestry and
Wildlife Sciences, Auburn University
Reading Adviser: Cecilia Minden-Cupp, PhD, Literacy Consultant

Photo Credits: Cover, pages 1 and 11, ©Bruce MacQueen, used under license from
Shutterstock, Inc.; page 5, ©James M Phelps, Jr, used under license from Shutterstock, Inc.;
page 7, ©Fotolistic, used under license from Shutterstock, Inc.; page 9 ©dragon_fang, used
under license from Shutterstock, Inc.; pages 13 and 15, ©Tony Campbell, used under license
from Shutterstock, Inc.; page 17, ©Gualberto Becerra, used under license from Shutterstock, Inc.;
page 19, ©PeterG, used under license from Shutterstock, Inc.; page 21, ©David Gallaher, used
under license from Shutterstock, Inc.

LIBRARY OF CONGRESS CATALOGING-IN-PUBLICATION DATA
Raatma, Lucia.
  How do we live together? Deer / by Lucia Raatma.
    p. cm.—(Community connections)
  Includes bibliographical references and index.
  ISBN-13: 978-1-60279-618-8
  ISBN-10: 1-60279-618-1
  1. Deer—Juvenile literature. I. Title. II. Title: Deer. III. Series.
  QL737.U55R33 2010
  599.65—dc22   2009023401

Cherry Lake Publishing would like to acknowledge the
work of The Partnership for 21st Century Skills. Please
visit www.21stcenturyskills.org for more information.

Printed in the United States of America
Corporate Graphics Inc.
January 2010
CLSP06

CONTENTS

DANGER ON THE ROAD

"Look out!" your dad yells. Your mom nods and drives slower. Your family is traveling on a busy street. There is a deer near the side of the road. Where did it come from? Why is it so close to moving cars?

Deer don't always know when cars are coming.

Many deer have lost their homes. Trees are often cut down when roads and houses are built. Deer try to reach other wooded areas. They sometimes cross busy roads. This is dangerous for both deer and people. Deer might be killed if cars hit them. People can also be badly hurt.

Road signs help people avoid hitting deer with their cars.

Many people think deer are pests. Deer may eat crops such as corn or apples. Farmers want them to stay away from their land.

Deer still have a right to use the outdoors. People need to find ways to get along with deer.

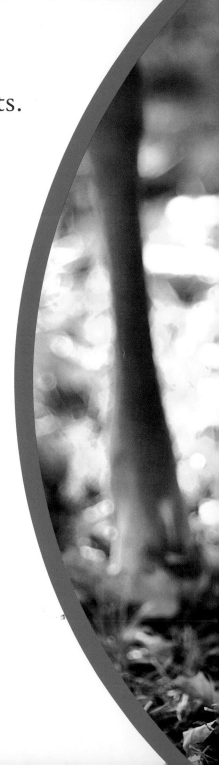

Apples are one of a deer's favorite foods.

Look around your neighborhood. Are there new homes or new stores? What used to be in those areas? Trees? Bushes? Have they all been cleared away? What kinds of animals might have lived there?

9

A CLOSER LOOK AT DEER

Have you ever seen deer in the wild? White-tailed deer are most common in North America. These **mammals** live throughout Canada, Mexico, and the United States. They live in many **habitats**, including forests and meadows.

White-tailed deer are a common sight for many people.

Adult male deer are usually called **bucks**. They have **antlers**. Their antlers fall off and grow again each year. Adult female deer are usually called **does**. Baby deer are often called **fawns**.

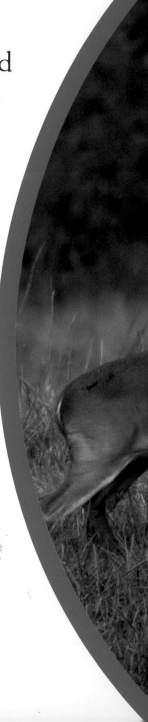

Male deer use their antlers to battle each other during mating season.

Antlers are bones.
They are hard. Can
you guess why most
males have antlers?
Antlers help deer
to stay safe from
enemies. Deer also
use their antlers to
fight other deer.

13

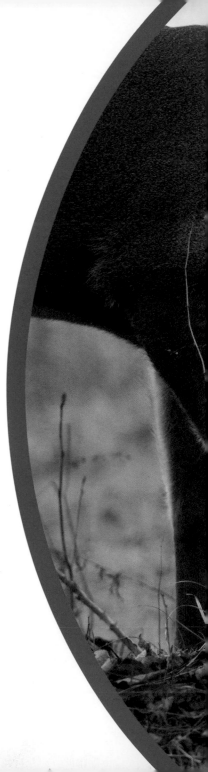

Deer enjoy eating many foods. Some favorites are corn, fruit, and **legumes**. They also like to eat leaves. They search for food in forests, countrysides, and neighborhoods.

Bucks sometimes rub their antlers on bushes and trees. This can hurt the plants.

Deer rub their antlers on trees as a way to mark their territory.

SHARING THE GREAT OUTDOORS

Imagine planting a garden of beans and other foods. How would you feel if deer ate your plants? Or picture being a farmer. What if your corn was eaten by deer? You would probably be upset! How can we control what deer eat? How can we live together?

Deer can quickly destroy a gardener's hard work.

People sometimes hunt deer to keep the population down. Not everyone agrees with this idea. They think it is wrong to kill animals.

Deer will jump over a low fence. So some people put up high fences to protect their yards. People also spray plants with things that deer won't like to eat. One example is hot sauce!

Fences help keep deer out of places where they don't belong.

Deer are most active at **dawn** and **dusk**. They often travel in groups. Drivers should slow down if they spot a deer. There may be more.

We must find ways to respect deer and live together. Remember, this world belongs to all of us!

Deer have a right to share our outdoor space!

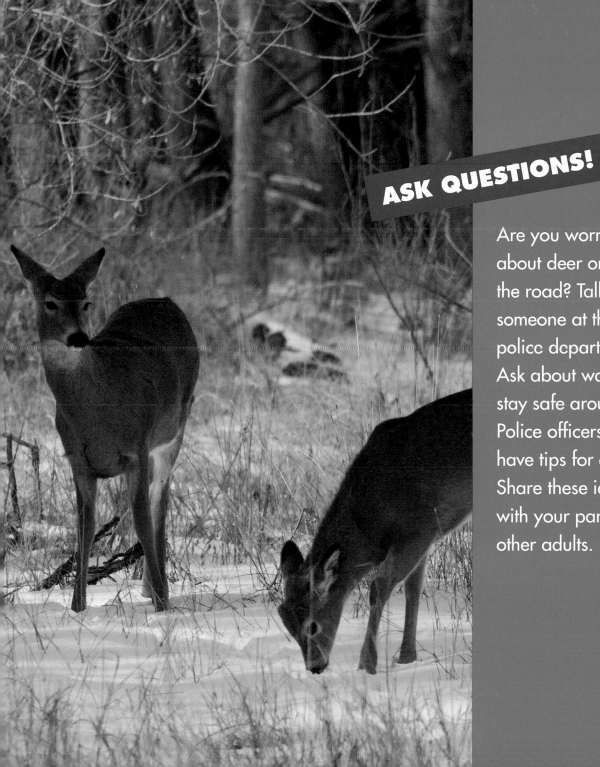

ASK QUESTIONS!

Are you worried about deer on the road? Talk to someone at the local police department. Ask about ways to stay safe around deer. Police officers might have tips for drivers. Share these ideas with your parents and other adults.

GLOSSARY

antlers (ANT-lurz) bony growths on a male deer's head

bucks (BUHKSS) adult male deer

dawn (DAWN) the first daylight of the morning

does (DOHZ) adult female deer

dusk (DUHSK) the time after sunset when it is almost dark

fawns (FAWNZ) baby deer

habitats (HAB-uh-tatss) the places and natural conditions in which plants and animals live

legumes (LEG-yoomz) plants with seeds that grow in pods

mammals (MAM-uhlz) warm-blooded animals that are usually covered in hair, have backbones, give birth to live young, and make milk to feed their babies

FIND OUT MORE

BOOKS

Macken, JoAnn Early. *Deer*. Pleasantville, NY: Gareth Stevens Publishing, 2010.

Nelson, Robin. *Deer*. Minneapolis: Lerner Publications, 2009.

WEB SITES

Animal Planet—Wild Animals A to Z: Deer
animal.discovery.com/mammals/deer/
Find facts about different kinds of deer.

National Geographic—Animals: White-Tailed Deer
animals.nationalgeographic.com/animals/mammals/white-tailed-deer.html
Learn more about these deer and hear how they sound through a brief audio clip.

INDEX

24

ABOUT THE AUTHOR

Lucia Raatma has written dozens of books for young readers. She and her family live in the Tampa Bay area of Florida. They think that little Key deer are beautiful.